The Magic School Bus®
PRESENTS
The Rain Forest

Scholastic Inc.

Photos ©: 123RF: 28 top left (Henner Damke), 29 bottom left (Noppharat Manaku), 28 bottom left (Oleksandr Dibrova), 8 top left (Peta Thames), 14 top left (Simone Van Den Berg); Alamy Images: 31 center right (Danita Delimont), 4 top left (Nick Gibson); Corbis Images: 9 (George Grall/National Geographic Society), 24 bottom center (Wayne Lynch/All Canada Photos); Dreamstime: 7 bottom right (Hotshotsworldwide), 3 center, 17 bottom right (Ika66), 8 bottom right (Noracarol), 3 top, 10 top left (Smileus), 13 bottom left (Weerachart Bunlungpho); Getty Images: 23 bottom center (Barry B. Doyle), 6 (Christer Fredriksson/Lonely Planet Images), 12 (David Maitland/Oxford Scientific), 8 center (Eco/UIG), 26–27 (Jacques Jangoux/Visuals Unlimited), 24 top left (johnstarkeyphotography), 1 (Kitchin and Hurst/All Canada Photos), 28 bottom right (Mary Plage/Oxford Scientific), 7 bottom left (Michael Melford/National Geographic Creative), 29 top left (Pete Oxford), 3 bottom, 22 (Steve Winter/National Geographic Creative); iStockphoto: cover center left (Kay in t Veen), 29 bottom right (skynavin), 21 center (TranceDrumer); Media Bakery/Theo Allofs: cover background; Minden Pictures: 23 center left (Pete Oxford), 19 (Piotr Naskrecki); Nature Picture Library: 28 top right (Axel Gomille), 10–11 (Bernard Walton), 17 bottom left (Dave Watts), 16 (Juan Carlos Munoz), 26 top left (Luiz Claudio Marigo), 4–5 (Lynn M. Stone), 18 center (Michael D. Kern), 29 top right (Nick Garbutt), 21 top right (Pete Oxford), 18 bottom right (Roland Seitre), 18 top left (Stephen Dalton), 14–15, 30 (Suzi Eszterhas), 25 (Tim Laman), 13 top right (Wegner/ARCO); Shutterstock, Inc.: cover bottom (DenisNata), cover bottom left and right (isarescheewin); Superstock, Inc.: 20 (Minden Pictures), 31 center left (National Geographic), 21 bottom left (Nature Picture Library).

ISBN 978-0-545-68585-6

Produced by Potomac Global Media, LLC

All text, illustrations, and compilation © 2015 Scholastic Inc.
Based on The Magic School Bus series © Joanna Cole and Bruce Degen
Text by Tom Jackson Illustrations by Carolyn Bracken
Consultant: Dr. Catherine Cardelus, Associate Professor of Biology, Colgate University

Published by Scholastic Inc., 557 Broadway, New York, NY 10012.

12 11 10 9 8 7 6 5 4 3 2 1   15 16 17 18 19 20

Cover design by Paul Banks
Interior design by Carol Farrar Norton
Photo research by Sharon Southren

Printed in the U.S.A.   40
First printing, January 2015

Contents

p. 10

p. 17

p. 22

In the Jungle

The classroom suddenly felt hot and sticky. "Time to get out of here," said Ms. Frizzle. "Let's head for the rain forest. It's a steamy jungle filled with amazing wildlife. Get ready for rain and lots of it!"

This photo of South America was taken from space. The green area is the Amazon rain forest. It is the largest rain forest in the world.

LET IT RAIN!

Rain forest air is full of water vapor. It feels like being in a bathroom after a hot shower.

In the jungle
The undergrowth is thick near streams and on hillsides where trees have fallen. It's hard to walk there, so people cut paths.

Packed tight
Rain forests are crowded with plants, especially along the banks of the many streams that flow through them.

Equator locator!

All about rain forests
by Wanda

Rain forests grow near the Equator—an imaginary line that scientists draw around the middle of Earth. It is always hot and sunny here. There are no summers or winters. The strong sunshine makes ocean water evaporate into rain clouds, and all this rain falls on the land, making rain forests grow.

Equator

■ = Rain forest

Frizzle Fact
One-fifth of all the world's rain falls in the Amazon rain forest and the area that surrounds it.

Plants need water and sunlight to survive. There is plenty of water in the rain forest, but not much light on the forest floor. The trees are very tall. They grow so close together that the branches at the top block out most of the light. Few plants grow on the forest floor.

Fighting for light.

All about forest plants
by Dorothy Ann

The plants in a rain forest grow in layers. Trees spread out at the top to create an upper layer of leaves called the canopy. The plants that grow beneath the canopy make up a lower layer called the understory. At the bottom, slow-growing plants and fungi grow in the gloom near the ground.

Canopy

Understory

Forest floor

Jungle tree trunk

Strong supports

Tall trees are supported by sturdy roots that grow out sideways. They make the trunk wider so the tree doesn't fall over easily.

Standing in water

It rains so much that a rain forest often floods. But the trees can keep growing in shallow water.

A sloth spends most of its life up a tree. It hangs on to branches using long, hook-shaped claws.

Jungle Plants

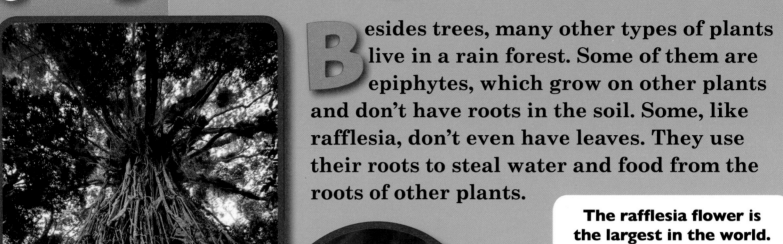

Besides trees, many other types of plants live in a rain forest. Some of them are epiphytes, which grow on other plants and don't have roots in the soil. Some, like rafflesia, don't even have leaves. They use their roots to steal water and food from the roots of other plants.

The rafflesia flower is the largest in the world. It grows to 90 centimeters (3 feet) wide.

The seeds of the strangler fig sprout at the top of a tree. Then its roots grow down to the ground.

Many rain forest plants have leaves with "drip spouts" so the rain pours off quickly. This keeps the leaves dry and stops mold growing in the warm, wet air.

The leaves of plants called bromeliads form a cup that collects the water they need. This frog has come for a drink.

Growing power!

How do rain forest plants survive?

by Phoebe

Plants make food by a process called photosynthesis. They take carbon dioxide gas from the air and water from the ground or air. Then they use sunlight to turn them into sugar. Plants growing on the dim rain forest floor grow very slowly because they don't get much light.

Most plants gather water from the ground using roots, but some rain forest plants don't have roots. Instead, they collect rainwater in their leaves or absorb it from the steamy jungle air.

African Apes

Rain forests are home to many different animal species. In Central Africa these include gorillas and chimpanzees. Both belong to a group of animals called apes. They are the closest living relatives to human beings. Gorillas are larger than humans—they weigh twice as much. Chimpanzees are a little bit smaller than humans, but are much stronger.

Gorillas roam the forest daily, looking for food. They eat leaves and flowers that grow on the forest floor.

Frizzle Fact

Before they go to sleep, chimps and gorillas make themselves comfortable beds out of leaves and branches.

Say cheese!

Chimp Expressions
by Dorothy Ann

Chimpanzees communicate with each other by using sounds and making faces. When a chimp sticks out its lips and makes an "ooh" sound, it's excited about something. Chimps also smile. If they show their teeth, they're in a playful mood. If they show their teeth and gums, it means they're scared. And if they open their mouths wide to show all their teeth, that means they're angry.

excited   playful   scared

Chimpanzees eat fruits and insects. They also work together to hunt small animals to eat.

Chimpanzees belong to groups, or troops, of about 50 apes. Most are mother chimps and their children.

Asian Apes

When it's too sunny, orangutans pull big leaves off trees to make shade.

Orangutans spend a lot of time alone, clambering through trees, looking for fruits and leaves to eat. Babies stay with their mothers until they are about seven years old.

Several types of apes live in the Southeast Asian rain forests of Indonesia and Malaysia. Asian apes spend their time high in the trees. The largest Asian ape is the orangutan. The smaller apes are all types of gibbons, including white-handed and crested gibbons.

The largest gibbon is called a siamang. It uses a stretchy bag in its throat to produce loud hooting calls.

Gibbons have very long arms. They use them to swing from one branch to the next.

Monkey business!

What are the differences between apes and monkeys?
by Ralphie

Many people describe chimps and other apes as monkeys. Although apes and monkeys are similar, they are not the same. The most obvious difference is that monkeys have a tail, while apes never do. Most monkeys are much smaller than apes, and they move by running and jumping. Apes have more flexible arms than monkeys. They use their arms to climb through trees and swing from branches.

Monkeys

The indri is a lemur. Lemurs are close relatives of monkeys.

Spider monkeys, howler monkeys, capuchins, tamarins, and marmosets are just a few types of rain forest monkeys. Many of them spend time high up in the canopy layer where they can escape predators. Others, like baboons, prefer life on the forest floor.

Frizzle Fact

Capuchin monkeys got their name because the dark fur on their heads reminded people of a capuchin monk's hood.

That's what I call smart!

All about monkeys
by Tim

Most monkeys eat fruits and leaves. Different trees grow shoots and fruits at different times, so monkeys have to remember where all the trees are and when to visit them. They also have to be able to act fast when under attack, since predators could strike from any direction. Making a bad jump or choosing the wrong place to land could be dangerous. All this means a monkey has to have a good memory and be able to make quick decisions.

Furry friends
Monkeys make friends by cleaning one another's fur.

Capuchin monkeys live in South and Central America. They often have cream-colored fur around the face and shoulders.

Bird Life

Wide wings
A macaw's wings are 4 feet (1.2 meters) across — as wide across as a bed.

Macaws are large parrots. They fly high above the forest, looking for fruit trees. They rip food apart with their powerful curved beaks.

Long tail
A macaw's tail is 36 inches (90 centimeters) long. That's half its length.

Macaws have strong toes. They use them to grab food and hold on to branches.

Frizzle Fact
The hooded pitohui bird of New Guinea has poisonous feathers. If you touch them, your hands go numb.

The rain forest is full of birds. Some live on the ground—like the cassowary in Australia and the red jungle fowl in India. Others, like macaws, fly up high in the treetops. Jungle birds are often very colorful so they can see one another among the leaves.

Why do parrots talk?
by Carlos

Parrots are famous for being able to talk. No one is exactly sure why they do this. The best explanation so far is that they learn to make calls in the wild by copying the sounds made by other parrots nearby. That means parrots in one part of the jungle make different calls than those living in other parts.

A pet parrot will copy the sounds of the people around it. After years of training and exposure to people, parrots can understand some words.

Largest jungle bird

Big head
The cassowary has a spike on its head that it uses to push its way through the undergrowth.

Jungle runner
Cassowaries do not fly, but can run very fast on their sturdy feet.

A toucan uses its huge beak to crack nuts. The beak makes up one-third of the bird's length.

17

Tree Frogs

F rogs can survive anywhere it's wet enough, so they are right at home in a rain forest. They climb through the trees, slurping up bugs. They never have to touch the ground. Even baby tadpoles swim in pools of water that form on large leaves.

A forest frog's skin is covered in slime, which stops it from drying out too quickly.

Flying frogs glide from one tree to the next. They have huge webbed hands and feet that act like parachutes.

These poison dart frogs have very strong poisons in their skin. Any animal that eats them will get very sick and may even die.

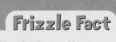
Frizzle Fact
The Goliath frog lives in the forests of Central Africa. It is the world's largest frog, weighing as much as a newborn baby!

Hop along!

What are the differences between a frog and a toad?
by Wanda

Both frogs and toads live in the jungle. There is no simple way of telling one from another. Toads normally live on the ground and have rough skin, short legs, and rounded heads. Frogs live in or near water. They have more pointed snouts and long legs. Frogs move by jumping, while toads generally walk or hop. But not all frogs and toads share these differences. In the end, frogs and toads belong to the same group of animals.

A tree frog has long legs with sticky pads on the tips of its toes. These pads help the feet grip as the frog climbs.

Jungle Bugs

Bird-eating spiders don't actually eat birds. But they do catch frogs and lizards.

The Goliath bird-eating spider lives in South America. It is the largest spider in the world. It could cover a dinner plate with its legs.

nsects and spiders can be found lurking everywhere in the rain forest. Thousands of different types of bugs live in the soil, on tree trunks, or at the tops of trees. Many of these jungle bugs are much bigger and tougher than in other parts of the world.

This rain forest beetle is armed with long horns. It uses them to fight other beetles and tries to knock them off branches.

It's a bug's world!

When the morpho butterfly flies through the trees, you can see flashes of the blue from the tops of its wings.

Leaf-cutter ants slice chunks out of leaves. They use the leaves to feed fungus, which the ants then eat.

How do scientists count bugs?
by Keesha

Scientists have found ways of counting bugs. Many flying insects are attracted to light. Scientists hang a sheet in the forest and put a powerful light behind it. When bugs land on the sheet, the scientists count the different types. They count the number of bugs in a tree by laying a sheet beneath it and using a machine to shake its trunk. It doesn't hurt the tree or the bugs, but all the bugs fall out and can be counted. One tree may be home to 1,500 bug species!

Jungle Giants

Tigers are the top predators in Asian rain forests. They are slightly bigger than African lions, which also makes them the biggest cats in the world.

Jungles are home to some big animals. They include elephants, rhinoceroses, forest hogs, and snakes. Many of these jungle giants are predators—and they also happen to be the largest of their kind anywhere in the world.

Size matters!

Being small
by Arnold

The rain forest is home to small animals, too. The pygmy marmoset is the world's smallest monkey. It is so tiny it could sit in the palm of your hand. The world's smallest frog is also a rain forest creature.

Small animals have to eat more often than big animals, but there's plenty of food in the forest. Being small makes it much easier to move around through all the rain forest trees and bushes. But being small can be dangerous, too—big animals like to eat small animals!

The anaconda is the world's largest and heaviest snake. It hunts in rivers that run through the jungles of South America. It likes to eat fish, turtles, and even crocodiles.

I hope they don't see me...

The harpy eagle is one of the largest birds in the Amazon. It is also the most powerful, swooping into treetops to snatch monkeys from branches.

Frizzle Fact

The Amazon is home to the world's largest otter. It is nearly 6 feet (1.8 meters) long.

Nighttime Forest

When night falls and the monkeys and other daytime animals find places to sleep, a whole new set of creatures comes out of hiding. These nighttime animals have excellent eyesight and use their sense of smell to stay safe and track down food.

A tree python has a heat sensor on its snout. This picks up warmth coming from a body, so the python can track down its prey in the dark.

Jaguars spend the day resting on high branches.

Jaguar

Hidden!
Patterned fur acts as camouflage. It looks like moonlight shining through trees. This means it can be difficult to spot a jaguar until it's too late.

Big bite
Jaguars have very powerful jaws. They kill prey by crushing an animal's head with their teeth.

Frizzle Fact
A bush baby is a type of primate. It leaves its scent on branches as it looks for food at night. It uses the scent to find its way back home.

Tarsiers are tiny relatives of monkeys. They have enormous eyes that catch enough light to see their insect prey in the dark.

Night, night.

Day and night in the forest
by Phoebe

Rain forests do not have seasons like other parts of the world. It is always hot. It rains all year, too, although there are some times when it rains more heavily. The biggest change in conditions in the forest is between night and day. Day is like the summer, when all the plants grow quickly. Night is like the winter — it gets a bit colder and the air is less steamy. While some animals can be active at any time, most jungle creatures prefer to live either in the dark or in the light.

Forest Destruction

Rain forests are home to half the world's plant and animal species. But they are often cut down to make way for farms and cities. Rain forests shrink each year as humans develop more land. More than half the world's rain forests have already been damaged or destroyed. Some forests are now protected by governments.

Rare forest animals, such as tamarin monkeys, have been bred in zoos and then reintroduced to safe places in the forest.

Frizzle Fact

Every year worldwide, an area of forest twice the size of Delaware is cut down.

Bad news!

Why can't rain forests grow back?
by Tim

Once a rain forest has been cut down, it is gone forever. Even if you let trees grow back, the forest will never be the same again.

Rain forests are ancient places. They have not changed much for millions of years. The wildlife that lives there is found nowhere else in the world, and it cannot survive without the forest. If the forest is destroyed, by the time new trees grow back, many of the original species will have died out.

Rain forests are often cleared using the slash-and-burn system. People cut down the trees and set fire to the logs.

Rain Forest Animals

Capybara

This animal lives in the rivers that run through the forests of South America. It is related to squirrels and rats, but grows to more than 4 feet (1.2 meters) long. It grazes on riverside plants but dashes into water to escape predators.

Flying fox

Flying foxes are actually large bats. They have wings made from skin stretched over their long finger bones. Flying foxes are fruit-eaters. They hang from their back legs when resting, and drop into the air when they want to fly away.

Sun bear

This is the world's smallest bear. It lives in the jungles of Southeast Asia. It has a long, rough tongue, which it uses to slurp up honey and insects it digs out of rotten wood. It gets its name because of a pale circular patch on its chest that looks like the Sun.

Javan rhinoceros

This very rare forest rhino has just one horn, while most other species of rhinoceros have two. It stays out of sight in the thick jungle undergrowth. When it's frightened, this rhino charges and uses its great weight (which is about the same as a car) to get away.

Well done, class! Let's get ready for our next adventure!

Ocelot

This little wild cat lives in South America. It is sometimes called a dwarf leopard because of its spotty

coat. Ocelots grow to about 4 feet (1.2 meters) long. They sleep in trees during the day and hunt at night, sniffing out mice, birds, and lizards. They even catch fish from rivers.

Violin beetle

This strangely shaped beetle's body is very flat. It can squeeze into cracks under bark and between layers of fungus that grow on forest trees. It preys on smaller

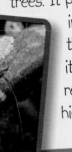

insects that live in the cracks, and uses its long flexible neck to reach them in their hiding places.

Malaysian tapir

Despite its trunklike nose, this species is more closely related to horses than to elephants. Its head

and shoulders are narrower than its rear end, giving it a wedge-shaped body. This helps the animal to push its way through the thick jungle undergrowth.

King cobra

This deadly snake is the longest venomous snake in the world. It preys on other snakes and its venom is powerful enough to kill an elephant. Before it strikes, the

snake lifts the front of its body straight up. A large cobra would be tall enough to look a grown man in the eye.

29

Saving the Rain Forest

It is important to look after rain forests because they are home to half of the world's plant and animal species. Most of them cannot survive anywhere else. Many rain forest plants have never been studied, but could be useful medicines in the future. Scientists are working with the people who live in rain forests to make sure more people see the forests' true value.

This jungle ranger records the behavior of some gorillas in an African rain forest.

❮ Conservationist

Scientists who look after wildlife are called conservationists. They figure out how the many animals and plants in a rain forest live together. Then they make sure that humans don't damage them or their environment. Conservationists make surveys of the jungle to see if any animals or plants are becoming rare. They come up with plans to make sure animals are protected in the future.

∨ Tour Guide

Looking after a rain forest can be an expensive business. One of the best ways to raise money is for people who live in the forest to take tourists on trips to see the amazing jungle. This way the forest people earn money to live without having

to clear the jungle to grow food. This kind of vacation is called ecotourism, and it helps the environment. Ecotourists come to see animals like parrots, sloths, gorillas, and tigers. They need to be able to get into the jungle, which means building roads and airports. Tourists also need comfortable hotels to stay in. Ecotourism experts have to make sure that all this building doesn't hurt the forest and its wildlife.

❯ Farmer

It is possible to grow food crops in a rain forest without having to cut down any of the trees. Rain forest farmers plant coffee beans and the cocoa beans that are used for making chocolate. Other rain forest crops include maize, nuts, pineapples, and other tropical fruits. Many of the products produced in rain forests have labels explaining that the money raised from selling them is used to find ways of protecting the rain forest and its wildlife.

Words to Know

Camouflage A disguise or natural coloring that allows animals to hide by blending in with their surroundings.

Carbon dioxide A gas that is a mix of carbon and oxygen, with no color or odor. People and animals breathe this gas out, while plants absorb it during the day.

Evaporate To change into a vapor or gas.

Fungus A plantlike organism with no leaves, flowers, or roots. It grows on other plants or decaying matter.

Jungle A forest in a tropical geographic area that is thickly covered with trees, vines, and bushes.

Photosynthesis A chemical process by which green plants and other organisms make their food. Plants use energy from the Sun to turn water and carbon dioxide into food. They produce oxygen for humans and animals to breathe.

Poisonous Having a poison that can harm or kill. Some snakes, insects, and even plants are poisonous.

Predator An animal that lives by hunting other animals for food.

Prey An animal that is hunted by another animal for food.

Primate Any member of the group of mammals that includes monkeys, apes, or humans.

Sensor A part of an animal that can detect and measure changes in the environment and transmit the information to the brain.

Slime A moist, soft, and slippery substance.

Species One of the groups into which animals and plants are divided by scientists. Members of the same species can mate and have offspring.

Venomous An animal that expels poison from its mouth.

Vine A plant with a long, twining stem that grows along the ground or climbs on trees.